New York Cheesecake Cookbook

Classic and Creative Recipes for the Perfect Cheesecake

NEW YORK CHEESECAKE COOKBOOK

First edition. November 17, 2023.

Written by john ahmad.

Table of Contents

John Ahmad

Chapter 1: Introduction to New York Cheesecake

History and origins of New York cheesecake

New York cheesecake holds a special place in the hearts of dessert enthusiasts worldwide. Its rich and creamy texture, velvety smoothness, and delightful tang make it a true dessert classic. In this chapter, let's explore the fascinating history and origins of New York cheesecake.

New York cheesecake has its roots in the late 19th century when European immigrants brought their traditional cheesecake recipes to America. However, it was in the vibrant culinary scene of New York City where this creamy delight truly flourished. The unique blend of cultures and influences in the city led to the development of the iconic New York-style cheesecake that we know today.

As the story goes, the New York-style cheesecake gained popularity thanks to a handful of iconic bakeries in New York City. Their mastery of the craft and the use of high-quality ingredients helped establish New York cheesecake as a dessert par excellence. Over the years, it became a symbol of indulgence and sophistication.

Key ingredients and equipment for making a perfect cheesecake

To create a New York-style cheesecake that will leave your taste buds singing, it's essential to use the right ingredients and equipment. Let's delve into the key components that contribute to the perfect cheesecake:

Cream Cheese: The star ingredient of New York cheesecake, cream cheese provides the rich and tangy flavor profile that sets it apart from other cheesecake varieties. It's crucial to choose a high-quality cream cheese with a smooth and creamy texture. Philadelphia cream cheese is a popular choice for its consistent quality and excellent results.

Sugar: Sweetness is crucial in balancing the tanginess of the cream cheese. Granulated sugar is typically used in New York cheesecake recipes, but some variations may incorporate brown sugar or a combination of sugars for added depth of flavor.

Eggs: Eggs play a crucial role in the texture and structure of the cheesecake. They provide richness and help bind the ingredients together. Large eggs are commonly used, but the recipe may specify otherwise.

Graham Cracker Crust: The traditional crust for New York cheesecake is made from graham crackers mixed with melted butter and a touch of sugar. The buttery and slightly sweet crust serves as a perfect base for the creamy filling. Other crust variations, such as cookie crusts or nut-based crusts, can also be used to add unique flavors and textures.

Vanilla Extract: Vanilla extract enhances the overall flavor of the cheesecake and complements the creamy notes. Use pure vanilla extract for the best results.

Lemon Zest: The addition of lemon zest provides a hint of brightness and freshness to the cheesecake. It adds a subtle citrusy aroma that beautifully complements the richness of the cream cheese.

Springform Pan: A springform pan is an essential tool for baking New York cheesecake. Its removable sides and bottom allow for easy and elegant release of the delicate dessert. The pan should be well-greased or lined with parchment paper to prevent the crust from sticking.

Water Bath: A water bath, also known as a bain-marie, is a technique used to bake the cheesecake gently and evenly. It involves placing the springform pan in a larger baking pan filled with hot water, which helps regulate the temperature and prevent the cheesecake from cracking during baking.

Tips for achieving a smooth and creamy texture

Creating a New York-style cheesecake with a smooth and creamy texture requires attention to detail and a few tried-and-true techniques. Here are some tips to help you achieve cheesecake perfection:

Ensure all ingredients are at room temperature before starting. This allows for easier blending and a smoother texture.

Beat the cream cheese until it is light and fluffy, making sure there are no lumps remaining. A stand mixer or hand mixer is ideal for this step.

Add the sugar gradually, mixing well after each addition. This helps the sugar dissolve and prevents graininess in the final cheesecake.

Beating the eggs in one at a time ensures even incorporation and a creamy texture. Mix on low speed until just combined to avoid incorporating excess air into the batter.

Avoid overmixing the batter once the flour and other ingredients are added. Overmixing can result in a dense and heavy cheesecake.

Use a water bath to bake the cheesecake. This gentle heat and moisture help prevent cracks and ensure even baking.

Once the cheesecake is baked, let it cool gradually. Start by removing it from the oven and allowing it to cool at room temperature for a while before transferring it to the refrigerator. This helps prevent cracking due to sudden temperature changes.

By following these tips and using high-quality ingredients, you'll be well on your way to creating a New York cheesecake with a velvety smooth and creamy texture that will impress your family and friends.

Now that we've covered the introduction to New York cheesecake, the history, key ingredients, and essential techniques, it's time to dive into the classic New York cheesecake recipe in Chapter 2. Get ready to tantalize your taste buds!

Chapter 2: Classic New York Cheesecake Recipes

In Chapter 2, we'll explore the classic New York cheesecake recipe that has been delighting dessert lovers for generations. We'll also dive into some exciting variations that add a creative twist to this timeless dessert. Additionally, we'll share valuable tips to help you achieve a crack-free top and avoid over-baking your cheesecake.

2.1 Traditional New York Cheesecake Recipe

The traditional New York cheesecake is a testament to simplicity and elegance. Its smooth and creamy texture, combined with a buttery graham cracker crust, creates a heavenly dessert. Let's take a look at the ingredients and steps involved in creating this iconic treat:

Ingredients:

- 2 cups graham cracker crumbs
- 1/2 cup unsalted butter, melted
- 4 (8 oz) packages of cream cheese, at room temperature
- 1 1/2 cups granulated sugar
- 4 large eggs
- 1 tsp vanilla extract
- 1 tsp lemon zest
- 1/2 cup sour cream

Instructions:

1. Preheat the oven to 325°F (163°C). Grease a 9-inch springform pan and wrap the bottom with aluminum foil to prevent any water from seeping in during the water bath.
2. In a bowl, combine the graham cracker crumbs and melted

butter. Press the mixture evenly into the bottom of the prepared pan to create the crust. Place it in the refrigerator while preparing the filling.

3. In a large mixing bowl, beat the cream cheese until smooth and creamy. Add the sugar gradually, mixing well after each addition until fully incorporated.

4. Add the eggs, one at a time, beating well after each addition. Scrape down the sides of the bowl as needed. Incorporate the vanilla extract and lemon zest.

5. Finally, add the sour cream and mix until just combined. Be careful not to overmix at this stage.

6. Remove the crust from the refrigerator and pour the cream cheese filling over it. Smooth the top with a spatula.

7. Place the springform pan in a larger baking pan. Carefully pour hot water into the larger pan, creating a water bath. The water should reach about halfway up the sides of the springform pan.

8. Bake in the preheated oven for about 60-70 minutes, or until the edges are set and the center is slightly jiggly. The cheesecake will continue to firm up as it cools.

9. Once baked, remove the cheesecake from the oven and let it cool in the water bath for 10 minutes. Then, carefully remove it from the water bath and allow it to cool completely on a wire rack.

10. Once completely cooled, refrigerate the cheesecake for at least 4 hours or overnight before serving. This will ensure the flavors meld together and the texture firms up.

2.2 Variations on the Classic Recipe

While the classic New York cheesecake is divine on its own, adding variations can elevate the dessert to new levels of indulgence. Here are a few exciting ideas to experiment with:

Chocolate Swirl: Create a marbled effect by swirling melted chocolate into the cream cheese filling before baking. Use a toothpick or skewer to gently swirl the chocolate for a beautiful pattern.

Raspberry-Infused: Blend fresh raspberries or raspberry puree into the cream cheese mixture for a burst of fruity flavor. You can also add a raspberry sauce or compote as a topping.

Oreo Cookie Crust: Substitute the graham cracker crust with crushed Oreo cookies mixed with melted butter. This twist adds a delightful chocolatey and cookie crunch to the cheesecake.

Salted Caramel Drizzle: Prepare a rich salted caramel sauce and drizzle it over the top of the baked and cooled cheesecake. The combination of sweet and salty flavors is irresistible.

Feel free to experiment and get creative with different flavors, such as lemon, strawberry, or even matcha, to put your own unique spin on the classic New York cheesecake.

2.3 Tips for Achieving a Crack-Free Top and Avoiding Over-Baking

A crack-free top is the hallmark of a perfectly baked New York cheesecake. Here are some tips to help you achieve that flawless appearance:

Use Room Temperature Ingredients: Ensure that the cream cheese, eggs, and sour cream are at room temperature before mixing them. This allows for easier blending and helps prevent lumps in the batter.

Avoid Overbeating: Mix the ingredients on low speed and avoid overbeating the batter. Overmixing can introduce too much air, leading to cracks during baking.

Water Bath Technique: Baking the cheesecake in a water bath helps regulate the oven's heat and keeps the cheesecake moist. The water bath prevents rapid temperature changes, reducing the chances of cracks.

Gradual Cooling: Once the cheesecake is baked, let it cool gradually. Start by removing it from the oven and allowing it to cool in the water bath for 10 minutes. Then, transfer it to a wire rack to cool completely at room temperature before refrigerating. Sudden temperature changes can cause cracks.

Don't Overbake: The cheesecake should be slightly jiggly in the center when you remove it from the oven. It will continue to set as it cools. Overbaking can result in a dry and cracked cheesecake.

By following these tips and techniques, you'll be well on your way to mastering the classic New York cheesecake and its variations. In the next chapter, we'll explore decadent cheesecake toppings and sauces that will take your cheesecake creations to new heights of deliciousness.

Chapter 3: Decadent Cheesecake Toppings and Sauces

In Chapter 3, we'll explore a variety of decadent toppings and sauces that elevate the flavor and presentation of New York cheesecake. From rich chocolate ganache to luscious fruit compotes and creamy sauces, these additions will take your cheesecake creations to the next level of indulgence. Get ready to tantalize your taste buds!

3.1 Rich Chocolate Ganache Topping

Chocolate lovers rejoice! A silky and velvety chocolate ganache is a perfect complement to the creamy texture of New York cheesecake. Here's a simple recipe to create a decadent chocolate ganache topping:

Ingredients:

- 8 oz semi-sweet or dark chocolate, finely chopped
- 1 cup heavy cream
- 1 tablespoon unsalted butter
- 1 teaspoon vanilla extract

Instructions:

1. Place the finely chopped chocolate in a heatproof bowl.
2. In a saucepan, heat the heavy cream over medium heat until it just starts to simmer. Be careful not to boil it.
3. Pour the hot cream over the chopped chocolate and let it sit for a minute to allow the chocolate to melt.
4. Gently whisk the mixture until smooth and glossy. Add the butter and vanilla extract, and whisk again until fully incorporated.
5. Allow the ganache to cool for a few minutes, until it thickens

slightly.

6. Pour the ganache over the chilled cheesecake, starting from the center and working your way to the edges. Let it cascade down the sides for an elegant presentation.

7. Refrigerate the cheesecake until the ganache sets, usually for about 30 minutes to an hour.

The luscious chocolate ganache will add a touch of decadence and a beautiful glossy finish to your New York cheesecake.

3.2 Fresh Fruit Compotes and Coulis

Fresh fruit compotes and coulis bring vibrant colors, natural sweetness, and refreshing flavors to your cheesecake. Here's a versatile recipe to create a delightful fruit topping:

Ingredients:

- 2 cups fresh or frozen fruits (such as strawberries, blueberries, raspberries, or peaches), diced or sliced
- 1/4 cup granulated sugar
- 1 tablespoon fresh lemon juice
- 1 teaspoon cornstarch (optional, for thickening)

Instructions:

1. In a saucepan, combine the diced or sliced fruits, granulated sugar, and lemon juice. Stir gently to coat the fruits with sugar.
2. Place the saucepan over medium heat and bring the mixture to a simmer. Let it cook for about 5-7 minutes, until the fruits soften and release their juices.
3. If you prefer a thicker consistency, mix the cornstarch with a small amount of water to create a slurry. Stir the slurry into the fruit mixture and cook for an additional minute until the sauce thickens slightly. Remove from heat.
4. Allow the fruit compote or coulis to cool to room temperature.
5. Spoon the compote or drizzle the coulis over the chilled cheesecake, covering the entire surface or creating artistic patterns.
6. For an extra touch, garnish with a few fresh fruit pieces on top.
7. The vibrant and tangy fruit compotes and coulis will add a burst of freshness and a visually stunning element to your cheesecake.

3.3 Caramel and Butterscotch Sauces

Caramel and butterscotch sauces lend a rich and buttery sweetness that pairs beautifully with New York cheesecake. Here's a simple recipe to create these delightful sauces:

Ingredients:

- 1 cup granulated sugar
- 1/4 cup water
- 1/2 cup heavy cream
- 2 tablespoons unsalted butter
- 1 teaspoon vanilla extract
- Pinch of salt

Instructions:

1. In a saucepan, combine the granulated sugar and water. Stir gently to moisten the sugar.
2. Place the saucepan over medium heat and let it come to a boil without stirring. Swirl the pan occasionally to ensure even heating.
3. Cook the sugar mixture until it turns a deep amber color, around 6-8 minutes. Be careful not to let it burn.
4. Remove the saucepan from heat and carefully pour in the heavy cream. The mixture will bubble vigorously, so exercise caution.
5. Stir the mixture until the cream is fully incorporated. Add the butter, vanilla extract, and salt, and stir until smooth and glossy.
6. Allow the caramel sauce to cool for a few minutes before using. It will thicken slightly as it cools.
7. Drizzle the caramel sauce generously over the chilled cheesecake. You can also create decorative patterns for an elegant presentation.
8. For butterscotch sauce, follow the same recipe, substituting brown sugar for granulated sugar. The result will be a rich and

indulgent butterscotch flavor that complements the creamy cheesecake perfectly.

3.4 Whipped Cream and Flavored Creams

Whipped cream adds a light and airy element to New York cheesecake, balancing the richness of the dessert. Here's a simple recipe to create homemade whipped cream:

Ingredients:

- 1 cup heavy cream, chilled
- 2 tablespoons powdered sugar
- 1 teaspoon vanilla extract

Instructions:

1. In a chilled mixing bowl, combine the heavy cream, powdered sugar, and vanilla extract.
2. Using an electric mixer or whisk, beat the cream on medium-high speed until soft peaks form. Be careful not to overbeat, as it can result in a grainy texture.
3. Spoon dollops of whipped cream onto individual slices of cheesecake or spread it evenly over the entire surface.

You can also experiment with flavored creams by adding extracts such as almond, mint, or coconut to the whipped cream. These flavored creams will add a delightful twist to your cheesecake creations.

Whether you choose rich chocolate ganache, vibrant fruit compotes, luscious caramel and butterscotch sauces, or a dollop of whipped cream, these decadent toppings and sauces will enhance the flavors and presentation of your New York cheesecake. In the next chapter, we'll explore the world of mini cheesecakes and individual portions, perfect for parties and gatherings. Get ready for bite-sized bliss!

Chapter 4: Mini Cheesecakes and Individual Portions

In Chapter 4, we'll explore the world of mini cheesecakes and individual portions. These delightful treats are perfect for parties, gatherings, or when you simply want a smaller portion of the classic New York cheesecake. We'll cover mini New York cheesecakes with various crust options, bite-sized cheesecake bars and squares, and creative presentation ideas to make your individual cheesecake servings truly special.

4.1 Mini New York Cheesecakes with Various Crust Options

Mini New York cheesecakes offer all the flavors and textures of the classic dessert in a perfectly portioned treat. You can get creative with different crust options to add unique flavors and textures. Here's a basic recipe to make mini New York cheesecakes, along with crust variations:

Ingredients:

- 1 1/2 cups graham cracker crumbs (or other crust options mentioned below)
- 1/4 cup unsalted butter, melted
- 16 oz cream cheese, at room temperature
- 1/2 cup granulated sugar
- 2 large eggs
- 1 tsp vanilla extract
- 1 tsp lemon zest
- 1/4 cup sour cream

Instructions:

1. Preheat the oven to 325°F (163°C). Line a muffin tin with paper liners or use individual silicone baking cups for easy

removal.

2. In a bowl, combine the graham cracker crumbs (or other crust options) and melted butter. Mix until the crumbs are evenly coated.

3. Spoon about 1 tablespoon of the crumb mixture into each liner or baking cup. Use the back of a spoon or your fingers to press the crumbs down firmly to create the crust.

4. In a mixing bowl, beat the cream cheese until smooth and creamy. Add the sugar gradually, mixing well after each addition.

5. Beat in the eggs, one at a time, followed by the vanilla extract and lemon zest. Finally, mix in the sour cream until just combined.

6. Spoon the cream cheese mixture into each crust-lined cup, filling almost to the top.

7. Bake for approximately 20-25 minutes, or until the cheesecakes are set and slightly jiggly in the center.

8. Remove from the oven and let them cool in the muffin tin or baking cups for about 10 minutes. Then, transfer them to a wire rack to cool completely.

9. Once cooled, refrigerate the mini cheesecakes for at least 2 hours or overnight before serving.

Crust Options:

Oreo Cookie Crust: Replace the graham cracker crumbs with crushed Oreo cookies mixed with melted butter for a chocolatey twist.

Nut Crust: Substitute graham cracker crumbs with finely crushed nuts (such as almonds or pecans) mixed with melted butter for added crunch and flavor.

Shortbread Crust: Crush shortbread cookies and mix them with melted butter for a buttery and crumbly crust.

4.2 Bite-Sized Cheesecake Bars and Squares

Another fantastic way to enjoy New York cheesecake is by creating bite-sized cheesecake bars and squares. They are easy to serve, portable, and perfect for any occasion. Here's a simple recipe to make bite-sized cheesecake bars:

Ingredients:

- 1 1/2 cups graham cracker crumbs
- 1/4 cup unsalted butter, melted
- 16 oz cream cheese, at room temperature
- 1/2 cup granulated sugar
- 2 large eggs
- 1 tsp vanilla extract
- 1 tsp lemon zest
- 1/4 cup sour cream

Instructions:

1. Preheat the oven to 325°F (163°C). Grease a square baking dish or line it with parchment paper for easy removal.
2. In a bowl, combine the graham cracker crumbs and melted butter. Mix until the crumbs are evenly coated.
3. Press the crumb mixture into the bottom of the prepared baking dish to create the crust.
4. In a mixing bowl, beat the cream cheese until smooth and creamy. Add the sugar gradually, mixing well after each addition.
5. Beat in the eggs, one at a time, followed by the vanilla extract and lemon zest. Finally, mix in the sour cream until just combined.
6. Pour the cream cheese mixture over the crust in the baking dish, spreading it evenly.
7. Bake for approximately 25-30 minutes, or until the cheesecake

is set and slightly jiggly in the center.

8. Remove from the oven and let it cool in the baking dish for about 10 minutes. Then, transfer it to a wire rack to cool completely.

9. Once cooled, refrigerate the cheesecake for at least 2 hours or overnight.

10. Cut the chilled cheesecake into bite-sized bars or squares before serving.

11. Bite-sized cheesecake bars and squares are perfect for serving at parties or as a delightful sweet treat for yourself or your guests.

4.3 Creative Presentation Ideas for Individual Cheesecake Servings

When it comes to serving individual cheesecakes, presentation is key. Here are a few creative ideas to make your individual cheesecake servings stand out:

Mason Jar Cheesecakes: Layer the crust, cream cheese filling, and toppings in small mason jars for a charming and portable dessert. You can screw on the lids to keep them fresh and serve with spoons.

Personalized Parfaits: Create individual cheesecake parfaits by layering crumbled graham cracker crust, cream cheese filling, and various toppings such as fruit compote, chocolate shavings, or whipped cream in small glasses or dessert cups.

Mini Cheesecake Sampler: Prepare a platter with an assortment of mini cheesecakes, each with a different flavor or topping. It allows guests to try various options and adds an element of fun to the dessert table.

Cheesecake Lollipops: Insert popsicle sticks into mini cheesecakes and dip them in melted chocolate or roll them in crushed nuts or cookie crumbs. These cheesecake lollipops make for a whimsical and easy-to-eat treat.

Cheesecake Bites in Phyllo Cups: Fill miniature phyllo pastry cups with bite-sized portions of cheesecake filling and top with a dollop of fruit preserves or a sprinkle of cinnamon. These elegant and bite-sized treats are perfect for upscale events.

Remember to garnish your individual cheesecake servings with fresh fruit, chocolate drizzle, whipped cream, or a dusting of powdered sugar to add that final touch of beauty and flavor.

With mini cheesecakes, bite-sized bars, and creative presentation ideas, you have a range of options to satisfy your guests' cravings or enjoy a perfectly portioned treat yourself. In the next chapter, we'll explore savory cheesecake creations that make for unique appetizers or brunch options. Get ready for a delightful twist on the classic cheesecake!

Chapter 5: Savory Cheesecake Creations

In Chapter 5, we'll venture into the realm of savory cheesecake creations. These delightful twists on the classic New York cheesecake incorporate herbs, spices, smoked salmon, bacon, and vegetables to create unique and flavorful appetizers or brunch options. Let's explore the savory side of cheesecakes!

5.1 Savory New York Cheesecake with Herbs and Spices

Who says cheesecake has to be sweet? A savory New York cheesecake infused with herbs and spices is a delicious and unexpected treat. The creamy and tangy flavors of the cheesecake pair beautifully with savory ingredients. Here's a recipe to get you started:

Ingredients:

- 2 cups plain bread crumbs
- 1/2 cup unsalted butter, melted
- 16 oz cream cheese, at room temperature
- 1 cup sour cream
- 3 large eggs
- 1/2 cup grated Parmesan cheese
- 2 tablespoons chopped fresh herbs (such as parsley, chives, or dill)
- 1 teaspoon garlic powder
- 1/2 teaspoon onion powder
- Salt and pepper to taste

Instructions:

1. Preheat the oven to 325°F (163°C). Grease a springform pan or a round baking dish.

2. In a bowl, combine the bread crumbs and melted butter. Press the mixture into the bottom of the prepared pan to create the crust.

3. In a mixing bowl, beat the cream cheese until smooth and creamy. Add the sour cream and continue mixing until well combined.

4. Add the eggs, one at a time, beating well after each addition. Incorporate the grated Parmesan cheese, chopped herbs, garlic powder, onion powder, salt, and pepper. Mix until all the ingredients are evenly distributed.

5. Pour the cream cheese mixture over the crust in the pan, spreading it evenly.

6. Bake for approximately 45-50 minutes, or until the cheesecake is set and slightly golden on top.

7. Remove from the oven and let it cool in the pan for about 10 minutes. Then, transfer it to a wire rack to cool completely.

8. Once cooled, refrigerate the cheesecake for at least 2 hours or overnight before serving.

9. Slice the savory cheesecake into wedges and serve as an appetizer or as part of a brunch spread. The combination of herbs and spices adds a savory depth of flavor that will surely impress your guests.

5.2 Cheesecake Bites with Smoked Salmon or Bacon

For an indulgent and savory twist, create cheesecake bites topped with smoked salmon or crispy bacon. These bite-sized treats are perfect for cocktail parties or as elegant appetizers. Here's how to make them:

Ingredients:

- Mini cheesecakes (prepared using the classic New York cheesecake recipe from Chapter 2 or any preferred savory variation)
- Smoked salmon slices or cooked bacon, chopped

- Fresh dill or chives for garnish

Instructions:

1. Prepare mini cheesecakes using the recipe and crust variation of your choice from Chapter 4.
2. Once the mini cheesecakes have cooled, remove them from their liners or baking cups and place them on a serving platter.
3. Top each mini cheesecake with a small piece of smoked salmon or a sprinkle of chopped crispy bacon.
4. Garnish with fresh dill or chives for added freshness and presentation.

These savory cheesecake bites with smoked salmon or bacon offer a delightful combination of flavors and textures, making them a standout appetizer at any gathering.

5.3 Vegetable-Infused Cheesecakes as Appetizers or Brunch Options

Adding vegetables to cheesecakes might sound unconventional, but it creates unique and delicious savory options. Here's a recipe for vegetable-infused cheesecakes that can be enjoyed as appetizers or as part of a brunch spread:

Ingredients:

- 2 cups crushed crackers or bread crumbs (such as Ritz crackers or panko breadcrumbs)
- 1/2 cup unsalted butter, melted
- 16 oz cream cheese, at room temperature
- 1 cup sour cream
- 3 large eggs
- 1 cup finely chopped mixed vegetables (such as spinach, bell peppers, onions, or mushrooms)
- 1/2 cup shredded cheddar or Swiss cheese

- 2 tablespoons chopped fresh herbs (such as parsley or chives)
- Salt and pepper to taste

Instructions:

1. Preheat the oven to 325°F (163°C). Grease a springform pan or a round baking dish.
2. In a bowl, combine the crushed crackers or bread crumbs and melted butter. Press the mixture into the bottom of the prepared pan to create the crust.
3. In a mixing bowl, beat the cream cheese until smooth and creamy. Add the sour cream and continue mixing until well combined.
4. Add the eggs, one at a time, beating well after each addition. Incorporate the finely chopped mixed vegetables, shredded cheese, chopped herbs, salt, and pepper. Mix until all the ingredients are evenly distributed.
5. Pour the cream cheese mixture over the crust in the pan, spreading it evenly.
6. Bake for approximately 45-50 minutes, or until the cheesecake is set and slightly golden on top.
7. Remove from the oven and let it cool in the pan for about 10 minutes. Then, transfer it to a wire rack to cool completely.
8. Once cooled, refrigerate the cheesecake for at least 2 hours or overnight before serving.
9. Slice the vegetable-infused cheesecake into squares or wedges and serve as an appetizer or as part of a brunch spread. The combination of vegetables, herbs, and cheese creates a savory and satisfying flavor profile.

Savory cheesecake creations offer a delightful departure from the sweet version, allowing you to explore unique flavors and textures. From savory herb-infused cheesecakes to bites topped with smoked salmon or bacon, and even vegetable-infused variations, these recipes are sure to impress and delight your guests. In the next chapter, we'll explore cheesecake-inspired desserts that will satisfy your sweet tooth. Get ready for a mouthwatering indulgence!

Chapter 6: Cheesecake-Inspired Desserts

In Chapter 6, we'll explore a range of cheesecake-inspired desserts that offer a delightful twist on the classic New York cheesecake. From cheesecake-stuffed cookies and brownies to creamy cheesecake ice cream and indulgent cheesecake parfaits and trifles, these desserts will satisfy your sweet tooth and take your love for cheesecake to new heights. Let's dive in!

6.1 Cheesecake-Stuffed Cookies and Brownies

Combining the rich flavors of cheesecake with the comforting goodness of cookies and brownies creates an irresistible treat. Here are two recipes to enjoy cheesecake-stuffed cookies and brownies:

Cheesecake-Stuffed Cookies:

Ingredients:

- 1 1/2 cups all-purpose flour
- 1/2 teaspoon baking soda
- 1/4 teaspoon salt
- 1/2 cup unsalted butter, softened
- 1/2 cup granulated sugar
- 1/2 cup packed brown sugar
- 1 large egg
- 1 teaspoon vanilla extract
- 8 oz cream cheese, softened
- 1/4 cup powdered sugar

Instructions:

1. Preheat the oven to 350°F (175°C). Line a baking sheet with parchment paper.

2. In a bowl, whisk together the flour, baking soda, and salt. Set aside.

3. In a separate bowl, cream together the softened butter, granulated sugar, and brown sugar until light and fluffy.

4. Add the egg and vanilla extract to the butter mixture, and beat until well combined.

5. Gradually add the flour mixture to the wet ingredients, mixing until just combined.

6. In another bowl, beat the cream cheese and powdered sugar until smooth and creamy.

7. Roll the cookie dough into small balls. Flatten each ball and place a teaspoon-sized dollop of the cream cheese mixture in the center. Fold the edges of the dough over the filling, sealing it completely.

8. Place the filled cookies on the prepared baking sheet, spacing them apart to allow for spreading.

9. Bake for about 12-15 minutes, or until the cookies are golden brown around the edges.

10. Remove from the oven and let the cookies cool on the baking sheet for a few minutes before transferring them to a wire rack to cool completely.

11. Enjoy these cheesecake-stuffed cookies as a delightful handheld treat.

Cheesecake-Stuffed Brownies:
Ingredients:

- 1 cup unsalted butter
- 2 cups granulated sugar
- 4 large eggs
- 1 teaspoon vanilla extract
- 1 cup all-purpose flour
- 1/2 cup unsweetened cocoa powder
- 1/4 teaspoon salt
- 8 oz cream cheese, softened
- 1/4 cup granulated sugar
- 1 large egg

Instructions:

1. Preheat the oven to 350°F (175°C). Grease a baking dish or line it with parchment paper.
2. In a saucepan, melt the butter over low heat. Remove from heat and stir in the granulated sugar.
3. Beat in the eggs, one at a time, followed by the vanilla extract.
4. In a separate bowl, whisk together the flour, cocoa powder, and salt.
5. Gradually add the dry ingredients to the butter mixture, stirring until just combined.
6. In another bowl, beat the cream cheese, granulated sugar, and egg until smooth and creamy.
7. Pour half of the brownie batter into the prepared baking dish, spreading it evenly.
8. Spoon the cream cheese mixture over the brownie batter. Spread it evenly, leaving a small border around the edges.
9. Pour the remaining brownie batter over the cream cheese layer, covering it completely.

10. Use a knife or toothpick to create swirls by gently running it through the layers.

11. Bake for approximately 30-35 minutes, or until a toothpick inserted in the center comes out with a few moist crumbs.

12. Remove from the oven and let the brownies cool completely in the baking dish before cutting them into squares.

These cheesecake-stuffed cookies and brownies are the perfect indulgence for cheesecake and dessert lovers alike.

6.2 Cheesecake Ice Cream and Milkshakes

Combining the creamy goodness of cheesecake with the cool and refreshing nature of ice cream and milkshakes creates a delightful treat for hot summer days. Here are two recipes to enjoy cheesecake ice cream and milkshakes:

Cheesecake Ice Cream:

Ingredients:

- 2 cups heavy cream
- 1 cup whole milk
- 1 cup granulated sugar
- 8 oz cream cheese, softened
- 1 teaspoon vanilla extract
- 1 cup crumbled graham crackers or crushed cookies (such as Oreos)
- Optional: additional mix-ins such as chocolate chips, fruit chunks, or caramel sauce

Instructions:

1. In a mixing bowl, combine the heavy cream, whole milk, and granulated sugar. Whisk until the sugar is dissolved.
2. In a separate bowl, beat the softened cream cheese until smooth and creamy.
3. Gradually pour the cream mixture into the cream cheese, whisking constantly until well combined.
4. Stir in the vanilla extract.
5. Pour the ice cream mixture into an ice cream maker and churn according to the manufacturer's instructions.
6. During the last few minutes of churning, add the crumbled graham crackers or crushed cookies, and any additional mix-ins if desired.
7. Once the ice cream reaches the desired consistency, transfer it

to a lidded container and freeze for a few hours or until firm.

8. Serve the cheesecake ice cream in bowls or cones and enjoy!

Cheesecake Milkshake:
Ingredients:

- 2 cups vanilla ice cream

- 1/2 cup milk
- 4 oz cream cheese, softened
- 1/4 cup powdered sugar
- 1 teaspoon vanilla extract
- Optional: whipped cream, crushed graham crackers, or a cherry for garnish

Instructions:

1. In a blender, combine the vanilla ice cream, milk, softened cream cheese, powdered sugar, and vanilla extract.
2. Blend until smooth and creamy, ensuring that the cream cheese is fully incorporated.
3. Pour the milkshake into a glass and garnish with whipped cream, crushed graham crackers, or a cherry if desired.
4. Serve immediately and enjoy the delicious cheesecake milkshake.
5. Cheesecake ice cream and milkshakes offer a refreshing and indulgent way to enjoy the flavors of cheesecake in frozen form.

6.3 Cheesecake Parfaits and Trifles

Layering cheesecake with complementary flavors and textures in parfaits and trifles creates visually stunning and utterly delicious desserts. Here's a recipe for a cheesecake parfait:

Cheesecake Parfait:
Ingredients:

- 1 cup graham cracker crumbs
- 2 tablespoons unsalted butter, melted
- 16 oz cream cheese, softened
- 1 cup powdered sugar
- 1 teaspoon vanilla extract
- 1 cup whipped cream
- Fresh berries or fruit compote for layering
- Optional: crushed graham crackers or cookie crumbs for topping

Instructions:

1. In a bowl, combine the graham cracker crumbs and melted butter. Mix until the crumbs are evenly coated.
2. In another bowl, beat the softened cream cheese, powdered sugar, and vanilla extract until smooth and creamy.
3. Gently fold in the whipped cream until well combined.
4. In serving glasses or dessert dishes, layer the graham cracker crumbs, cream cheese mixture, and fresh berries or fruit compote. Repeat the layers as desired.
5. Finish with a dollop of the cream cheese mixture on top and sprinkle with crushed graham crackers or cookie crumbs if desired.
6. Refrigerate the cheesecake parfaits for at least 2 hours before serving to allow the flavors to meld together.

These cheesecake parfaits can be prepared ahead of time and are perfect for elegant dinner parties or special occasions. The layers of creamy cheesecake, graham cracker crumbs, and vibrant fruit create a delightful combination of flavors and textures.

Feel free to get creative and experiment with different ingredients and flavors to make cheesecake trifles by layering cake, fruits, custard, or whipped cream along with the cheesecake mixture.

With cheesecake-stuffed cookies and brownies, cheesecake ice cream and milkshakes, and the elegant cheesecake parfaits and trifles, you have a range of delightful cheesecake-inspired desserts to enjoy. Indulge in these sweet treats and let your love for cheesecake shine through. In the next chapter, we'll explore tips for serving, storing, and preserving the freshness of your cheesecakes. Get ready to become a cheesecake connoisseur!

Chapter 7: No-Bake Cheesecake Delights

In Chapter 7, we'll explore the world of no-bake cheesecake delights. These recipes offer a quick and hassle-free way to enjoy the creamy and luscious flavors of New York cheesecake without the need for baking. From easy no-bake New York cheesecake to delectable cheesecake bars and squares, as well as chilled cheesecake desserts perfect for warm weather, these recipes will keep you cool and satisfied. Let's dive in!

7.1 Easy No-Bake New York Cheesecake Recipe

No-bake cheesecakes are a breeze to make and require minimal effort. Here's an easy recipe for a classic no-bake New York cheesecake:

Ingredients:

- 2 cups graham cracker crumbs
- 1/2 cup unsalted butter, melted
- 16 oz cream cheese, softened
- 1 cup powdered sugar
- 1 teaspoon vanilla extract
- 1 cup heavy cream

Instructions:

1. In a bowl, combine the graham cracker crumbs and melted butter. Mix until the crumbs are evenly coated.
2. Press the crumb mixture into the bottom of a springform pan to create the crust. Place it in the refrigerator to chill while preparing the filling.
3. In a mixing bowl, beat the softened cream cheese until smooth and creamy.

4. Add the powdered sugar and vanilla extract to the cream cheese, and continue mixing until well combined.
5. In a separate bowl, whip the heavy cream until stiff peaks form.
6. Gently fold the whipped cream into the cream cheese mixture until well incorporated.
7. Pour the filling onto the chilled crust in the springform pan, spreading it evenly.
8. Smooth the top with a spatula and refrigerate the cheesecake for at least 4 hours or until set.
9. Once set, remove the sides of the springform pan and transfer the cheesecake to a serving platter.
10. Slice and serve the easy no-bake New York cheesecake chilled for a delightful and fuss-free dessert experience.

7.2 No-Bake Cheesecake Bars and Squares

No-bake cheesecake bars and squares offer a convenient way to enjoy individual portions of creamy goodness. Here's a recipe for no-bake cheesecake bars:

Ingredients:

- 2 cups graham cracker crumbs
- 1/2 cup unsalted butter, melted
- 16 oz cream cheese, softened
- 1 cup powdered sugar
- 1 teaspoon vanilla extract
- 1 cup whipped cream
- Fresh berries or fruit compote for topping

Instructions:

1. In a bowl, combine the graham cracker crumbs and melted butter. Mix until the crumbs are evenly coated.
2. Press the crumb mixture into the bottom of a square baking

dish to create the crust. Place it in the refrigerator to chill while preparing the filling.

3. In a mixing bowl, beat the softened cream cheese until smooth and creamy.
4. Add the powdered sugar and vanilla extract to the cream cheese, and continue mixing until well combined.
5. Gently fold the whipped cream into the cream cheese mixture until well incorporated.
6. Pour the filling onto the chilled crust in the baking dish, spreading it evenly.
7. Smooth the top with a spatula and refrigerate the cheesecake bars for at least 4 hours or until set.
8. Once set, cut the cheesecake into individual bars and serve.
9. Top each cheesecake bar with fresh berries or fruit compote for a burst of flavor and added freshness.
10. No-bake cheesecake bars and squares are perfect for parties, picnics, or when you crave a quick and satisfying sweet treat.

7.3 Chilled Cheesecake Desserts for Warm Weather

When the weather heats up, chilled cheesecake desserts provide a refreshing and cool indulgence. Here's a recipe for a chilled cheesecake parfait:

Chilled Cheesecake Parfait:

Ingredients:

- 1 cup graham cracker crumbs
- 2 tablespoons unsalted butter, melted
- 16 oz cream cheese, softened
- 1 cup powdered sugar
- 1 teaspoon vanilla extract
- 1 cup whipped cream
- Fresh berries or fruit compote for layering
- Optional: crushed graham crackers or cookie crumbs for topping

Instructions:

1. In a bowl, combine the graham cracker crumbs and melted butter. Mix until the crumbs are evenly coated.
2. In another bowl, beat the softened cream cheese until smooth and creamy.
3. Add the powdered sugar and vanilla extract to the cream cheese, and continue mixing until well combined.
4. Gently fold the whipped cream into the cream cheese mixture until well incorporated.
5. In serving glasses or dessert dishes, layer the graham cracker crumbs, cream cheese mixture, and fresh berries or fruit compote. Repeat the layers as desired.
6. Finish with a dollop of the cream cheese mixture on top and sprinkle with crushed graham crackers or cookie crumbs if desired.

7. Refrigerate the cheesecake parfaits for at least 2 hours or until chilled.

Chilled cheesecake parfaits are a delightful and cooling dessert option for warm weather. The layers of creamy cheesecake, graham cracker crumbs, and vibrant fruit provide a burst of flavor and texture.

Feel free to get creative and experiment with different ingredients and flavors for chilled cheesecake desserts. You can incorporate crushed cookies, chocolate shavings, or even layers of flavored gelatin for added variety and visual appeal.

With easy no-bake New York cheesecake, no-bake cheesecake bars and squares, and chilled cheesecake desserts, you have a range of delicious options to satisfy your cheesecake cravings without turning on the oven. Enjoy these cool and creamy treats and beat the heat in style. In the next chapter, we'll explore tips for serving, storing, and preserving the freshness of your cheesecakes. Get ready to become a cheesecake connoisseur!

Chapter 8: Cheesecake for Special Occasions

In Chapter 8, we'll delve into the realm of cheesecake for special occasions. Cheesecakes can be transformed into stunning desserts perfect for holidays, weddings, and other celebrations. We'll explore holiday-themed cheesecakes, cheesecake wedding cakes and celebration centerpieces, as well as provide tips for decorating and garnishing cheesecakes to make them the highlight of any special event. Let's get started!

8.1 Holiday-Themed Cheesecakes

Holidays provide the perfect opportunity to infuse your cheesecakes with seasonal flavors and spices. Here are a few holiday-themed cheesecake ideas to tantalize your taste buds:

Pumpkin Spice Cheesecake:

Create a festive fall dessert by adding pumpkin puree, warm spices like cinnamon, nutmeg, and ginger to your cheesecake mixture. Top it off with a dollop of whipped cream and a sprinkle of pumpkin pie spice for a delightful pumpkin spice cheesecake.

Peppermint Cheesecake:

Capture the essence of the holiday season with a refreshing peppermint cheesecake. Add peppermint extract to your cream cheese filling and garnish with crushed candy canes or chocolate shavings. The combination of creamy cheesecake and cool mint will leave your taste buds in bliss.

Gingerbread Cheesecake:

Infuse the flavors of gingerbread into your cheesecake by incorporating molasses, ground ginger, cinnamon, and cloves. Create a gingerbread crust using crushed gingerbread cookies or graham crackers mixed with melted butter. Decorate the top with gingerbread cookie crumbs or a drizzle of spiced caramel sauce.

These holiday-themed cheesecakes are sure to bring joy and excitement to your festive celebrations.

8.2 Cheesecake Wedding Cakes and Celebration Centerpieces

Cheesecake wedding cakes and celebration centerpieces offer a unique and delicious alternative to traditional cakes. Here are some considerations and tips if you're planning to feature a cheesecake as the centerpiece for your special occasion:

Tiered Cheesecake Wedding Cakes: Create a show-stopping wedding cake by stacking multiple cheesecakes of varying sizes on top of one another. Use a sturdy support system between each layer to ensure stability. Decorate the cake with piped cream cheese frosting, fresh flowers, or edible pearls for an elegant touch.

Mini Cheesecake Tower: For a more casual or intimate celebration, consider a mini cheesecake tower. Prepare individual mini cheesecakes and arrange them in a tiered fashion on a decorative stand. Customize the flavors and decorations to suit your theme or color scheme.

Centerpiece Cheesecake: A single, large cheesecake can serve as a beautiful centerpiece for any celebration. Decorate it with edible flowers, fresh fruit, chocolate drizzle, or personalized cake toppers to match the occasion. Surround the cheesecake with additional bite-sized treats or a variety of flavored sauces for guests to enjoy.

Remember to consider any special dietary needs or restrictions of your guests when planning your cheesecake wedding cake or celebration centerpiece. Offering a variety of flavors, such as classic New York, fruity variations, and chocolate-infused options, ensures there's something for everyone to enjoy.

8.3 Tips for Decorating and Garnishing Cheesecakes for Special Events

When it comes to decorating and garnishing cheesecakes for special events, attention to detail can elevate their visual appeal. Here are some tips to make your cheesecakes shine:

Whipped Cream and Fresh Fruit: A classic and simple way to enhance the appearance of your cheesecake is by topping it with a generous dollop of freshly whipped cream and a selection of seasonal fresh fruits. This adds a touch of freshness and color to the dessert.

Chocolate Drizzle: For an elegant touch, drizzle melted chocolate or ganache over the top of your cheesecake. Use a spoon or a piping bag to create intricate patterns or write personalized messages. You can also sprinkle crushed nuts or edible gold dust for added texture and glamour.

Edible Flowers: Adorn your cheesecake with edible flowers, such as pansies, violets, or marigolds, to create a visually stunning dessert. Ensure the flowers are safe for consumption and free from pesticides. Gently place them on top of the cheesecake or use them as a garnish around the serving platter.

Personalized Cake Toppers: Add a personal touch to your cheesecake by incorporating custom cake toppers. These can be monogrammed initials, figurines representing the couple or the theme of the event, or even edible photo prints that capture cherished memories.

Creative Crusts: Experiment with different crust options to enhance the visual appeal of your cheesecake. Consider using crushed cookies, chocolate wafer crumbs, or even colored graham cracker crumbs for a unique and eye-catching crust.

Remember to consider the overall theme, color scheme, and style of your event when selecting decorations and garnishes for your cheesecake. Let your creativity shine through to create a dessert that not only tastes amazing but also looks stunning.

With holiday-themed cheesecakes, cheesecake wedding cakes and celebration centerpieces, as well as tips for decorating and garnishing cheesecakes, you're equipped to make any special occasion truly memorable. Let your cheesecakes take center stage and delight your guests with their exquisite flavors and stunning presentation. In the next chapter, we'll explore tips for serving, storing, and preserving the freshness of your cheesecakes. Get ready to become a cheesecake connoisseur!

Chapter 9: Cheesecake from Around the World

In Chapter 9, we'll embark on a delicious journey exploring cheesecake variations from different parts of the world. Cheesecake has been adapted and transformed in various culinary traditions, each offering its own unique twist and flavor profile. We'll dive into Japanese-style cotton cheesecake, Italian ricotta cheesecake, German-style cheesecake with quark filling, and other global adaptations that will broaden your cheesecake horizons. Let's explore the diverse world of cheesecake!

9.1 Japanese-Style Cotton Cheesecake

Japanese-style cotton cheesecake, also known as Japanese soufflé cheesecake, is renowned for its incredibly light, fluffy, and delicate texture. It's a delightful fusion of the classic New York cheesecake and a soufflé. Here's an overview of how to make this Japanese delicacy:

Ingredients:

- 7 oz cream cheese, softened
- 4 oz unsalted butter
- 1/2 cup milk
- 6 large eggs, separated
- 3/4 cup granulated sugar
- 1/2 cup all-purpose flour
- 1/4 cup cornstarch
- 1 teaspoon vanilla extract
- Confectioners' sugar for dusting (optional)

Instructions:

1. Preheat the oven to 325°F (163°C). Grease a round cake pan

and line the bottom with parchment paper.

2. In a heatproof bowl, melt the cream cheese, butter, and milk together over a double boiler or in short bursts in the microwave. Stir until smooth and well combined. Set aside to cool slightly.

3. In a large mixing bowl, beat the egg yolks and granulated sugar together until pale and creamy. Add the cream cheese mixture and whisk until smooth.

4. Sift the flour and cornstarch into the cream cheese mixture and whisk until well combined. Stir in the vanilla extract.

5. In a separate bowl, beat the egg whites until stiff peaks form.

6. Gently fold one-third of the beaten egg whites into the cream cheese mixture to lighten it. Then, fold in the remaining egg whites until no streaks remain.

7. Pour the batter into the prepared cake pan and smooth the top with a spatula.

8. Place the cake pan in a larger baking dish filled with hot water, creating a water bath.

9. Bake for approximately 60-70 minutes, or until the top is golden brown and the center is set but still slightly jiggly.

10. Remove from the oven and let it cool in the pan for about 10 minutes. Then, transfer it to a wire rack to cool completely.

11. Once cooled, dust the top with confectioners' sugar if desired.

Japanese-style cotton cheesecake is best enjoyed chilled. Its ethereal texture and subtle sweetness make it a beloved dessert in Japan and around the world.

9.2 Italian Ricotta Cheesecake

Italian ricotta cheesecake, or "torta di ricotta," is a delightful variation that features creamy ricotta cheese as the star ingredient. It has a lighter and more delicate texture compared to the denser New York-style cheesecake. Here's an overview of how to make Italian ricotta cheesecake:

Ingredients:

- 1 1/2 lbs ricotta cheese
- 1 cup granulated sugar
- 4 large eggs
- 1 teaspoon vanilla extract
- Zest of 1 lemon
- 1/4 cup all-purpose flour
- 1/4 cup semolina flour (optional, for added texture)
- Pinch of salt

Instructions:

1. Preheat the oven to 325°F (163°C). Grease a springform pan and line the bottom with parchment paper.
2. In a large mixing bowl, beat the ricotta cheese and sugar together until smooth and creamy.
3. Add the eggs one at a time, beating well after each addition.
4. Stir in the vanilla extract, lemon zest, all-purpose flour, semolina flour (if using), and a pinch of salt. Mix until all the ingredients are well combined.
5. Pour the batter into the prepared springform pan and smooth the top with a spatula.
6. Bake for approximately 60-70 minutes, or until the top is lightly golden and the center is set.
7. Remove from the oven and let it cool in the pan for about 10 minutes. Then, transfer it to a wire rack to cool completely.
8. Once cooled, refrigerate the cheesecake for at least 4 hours or overnight before serving.

Italian ricotta cheesecake is known for its delicate flavor and creamy texture. It pairs wonderfully with fresh fruit or a dusting of powdered sugar.

9.3 German-Style Cheesecake with Quark Filling

German-style cheesecake, or "Käsekuchen," is a beloved dessert in Germany and neighboring European countries. It features a filling made with quark, a type of soft cheese with a tangy flavor. Here's an overview of how to make German-style cheesecake:

Ingredients:

- 2 1/2 cups all-purpose flour
- 1/2 cup granulated sugar
- 1/2 teaspoon baking powder
- 1/2 cup unsalted butter, cold and cut into small pieces
- 1 large egg
- Pinch of salt
- 32 oz quark cheese (can substitute with a mixture of cream cheese and Greek yogurt)
- 1 cup granulated sugar
- 3 large eggs
- 1 teaspoon vanilla extract
- Zest of 1 lemon

Instructions:

1. Preheat the oven to 350°F (175°C). Grease a springform pan and line the bottom with parchment paper.
2. In a mixing bowl, combine the flour, sugar, baking powder, cold butter pieces, egg, and a pinch of salt. Mix until the mixture resembles coarse crumbs.
3. Press two-thirds of the crumb mixture into the bottom of the prepared springform pan to create the crust. Set aside the remaining crumb mixture.
4. In another bowl, beat the quark cheese, sugar, eggs, vanilla extract, and lemon zest together until smooth and well combined.

5. Pour the quark filling over the crust in the springform pan, spreading it evenly.
6. Sprinkle the remaining crumb mixture over the top of the quark filling, creating a crumbly topping.
7. Bake for approximately 50-60 minutes, or until the top is golden brown and the center is set.
8. Remove from the oven and let it cool in the pan for about 10 minutes. Then, transfer it to a wire rack to cool completely.
9. Once cooled, refrigerate the cheesecake for at least 4 hours or overnight before serving.

German-style cheesecake with quark filling offers a delightful tanginess and a crumbly texture that is loved by cheesecake enthusiasts around the world.

9.4 Other Global Variations and Adaptations

Cheesecake has been adapted and transformed in various culinary traditions across the globe. Here are a few more notable variations:

Greek-style cheesecake: Known as "tiropita," Greek cheesecake features a phyllo pastry crust filled with a mixture of feta cheese, eggs, and herbs.

French-style cheesecake: The French version, called "gâteau au fromage," often incorporates cream cheese and yogurt into the filling for a lighter texture.

Brazilian-style cheesecake: "Cuca de Queijo" is a Brazilian adaptation that blends cream cheese with tapioca starch, creating a slightly chewy and gluten-free texture.

Swedish-style cheesecake: "Ostkaka" is a Swedish delicacy made from cottage cheese or quark, flavored with almonds and served with lingonberry sauce.

These are just a few examples of how cheesecake has evolved and taken on unique characteristics in different culinary traditions. Exploring global adaptations allows you to appreciate the versatility and creativity behind this beloved dessert.

With Japanese-style cotton cheesecake, Italian ricotta cheesecake, German-style cheesecake with quark filling, and other global variations, you now have a broader understanding of cheesecake's diverse world. Each variation offers its own distinct flavors and textures, showcasing the creativity and cultural influences that shape this delightful dessert. In the next chapter, we'll explore tips for serving, storing, and preserving the freshness of your cheesecakes.

Chapter 10: Vegan and Dairy-Free Cheesecake Alternatives

In Chapter 10, we'll explore a variety of vegan and dairy-free alternatives to traditional cheesecake. These alternatives are perfect for individuals who follow a plant-based diet or have dietary restrictions. We'll delve into a plant-based New York cheesecake recipe, dairy-free crust options, and nut-based and tofu-based cheesecake alternatives that are sure to satisfy your cheesecake cravings without compromising on flavor. Let's dive in!

10.1 Plant-Based New York Cheesecake

Indulge in the creamy goodness of New York cheesecake with a plant-based twist. This recipe replaces traditional dairy ingredients with plant-based alternatives while maintaining the luscious texture and rich flavors you love. Here's an overview of how to make a plant-based New York cheesecake:

Ingredients:

For the crust:

- 1 1/2 cups graham cracker crumbs (ensure they are dairy-free)
- 1/4 cup melted coconut oil or vegan butter

For the filling:

- 16 oz vegan cream cheese
- 1 cup raw cashews, soaked overnight and drained
- 3/4 cup canned coconut cream
- 1/2 cup maple syrup or agave nectar
- 1/4 cup lemon juice
- 1 teaspoon vanilla extract

Instructions:

1. Preheat the oven to 325°F (163°C). Grease a springform pan and line the bottom with parchment paper.
2. In a bowl, combine the graham cracker crumbs and melted coconut oil or vegan butter. Mix until the crumbs are evenly coated. Press the crumb mixture into the bottom of the prepared springform pan to create the crust.
3. In a high-speed blender or food processor, blend the vegan cream cheese, soaked cashews, coconut cream, maple syrup or agave nectar, lemon juice, and vanilla extract until smooth and creamy.
4. Pour the filling onto the crust in the springform pan, spreading it evenly.
5. Bake for approximately 50-60 minutes, or until the top is set but still slightly jiggly.
6. Remove from the oven and let it cool in the pan for about 10 minutes. Then, transfer it to a wire rack to cool completely.
7. Once cooled, refrigerate the cheesecake for at least 4 hours or overnight before serving.

Plant-based New York cheesecake offers the same velvety texture and rich flavors as the traditional version while being free from dairy products.

10.2 Dairy-Free Crust Options

The crust is an essential element of cheesecake and can be easily adapted to be dairy-free. Here are a few options for creating a delicious dairy-free crust:

Graham Cracker Crust: Use dairy-free graham crackers or substitute them with a combination of crushed dairy-free cookies or gluten-free alternatives like almond meal or crushed gluten-free graham crackers.

Oat and Nut Crust: Combine ground oats, nuts (such as almonds or walnuts), a sweetener of your choice, and a binding agent like coconut oil or nut butter to create a flavorful and gluten-free crust.

Date and Nut Crust: Blend pitted dates and nuts (such as almonds or cashews) in a food processor until they form a sticky mixture. Press this mixture into the bottom of the springform pan to create a naturally sweet and nutrient-rich crust.

These dairy-free crust options provide a delicious foundation for your vegan or dairy-free cheesecake, adding a delightful crunch and complementary flavors to your dessert.

10.3 Nut-Based and Tofu-Based Cheesecake Alternatives

Nut-based and tofu-based cheesecake alternatives are excellent dairy-free options that offer creamy textures and unique flavors. Here are two alternatives to explore:

Nut-Based Cheesecake: Blend soaked raw cashews or macadamia nuts with coconut cream, sweeteners, and flavorings of your choice until smooth and creamy. This creates a luscious and rich filling that closely resembles traditional cheesecake.

Tofu-Based Cheesecake: Silken tofu can be used as a base for a creamy and smooth cheesecake filling. Blend silken tofu with sweeteners, lemon juice, and other flavorings to achieve a velvety texture similar to traditional cheesecake.

Both nut-based and tofu-based cheesecake alternatives allow you to enjoy the creamy goodness of cheesecake while providing a satisfying and dairy-free experience.

Experiment with different flavors, such as adding fruit purees, chocolate, or spices, to customize your vegan or dairy-free cheesecake alternatives and create unique and delectable desserts.

With a plant-based New York cheesecake recipe, dairy-free crust options, and nut-based and tofu-based cheesecake alternatives, you can indulge in cheesecake while adhering to your dietary preferences and restrictions. These alternatives offer a delightful and satisfying experience, ensuring that everyone can enjoy the pleasures of cheesecake.

Chapter 11: Gluten-Free and Grain-Free Cheesecake Options

In Chapter 11, we'll explore a range of gluten-free and grain-free alternatives for cheesecake. These options are perfect for individuals following a gluten-free diet or those seeking grain-free alternatives. We'll delve into gluten-free crust alternatives such as almond flour and gluten-free cookies, as well as grain-free cheesecake variations using coconut flour and nut crusts. Get ready to enjoy delicious cheesecake without the presence of gluten or grains. Let's get started!

11.1 Gluten-Free Crust Alternatives

For individuals who follow a gluten-free diet, there are several crust alternatives available that provide a delightful base for your cheesecake. Here are a few gluten-free crust options:

Almond Flour Crust:

Replace traditional graham crackers with almond flour to create a gluten-free crust. Combine almond flour, melted butter or a dairy-free alternative, and a sweetener of your choice. Press the mixture into the bottom of the springform pan to create a delicious and gluten-free crust.

Gluten-Free Cookie Crust:

Choose your favorite gluten-free cookies, such as gluten-free graham crackers or gluten-free shortbread cookies. Crush them into crumbs and combine them with melted butter or a dairy-free alternative. Press the mixture into the bottom of the pan to create a flavorful and gluten-free crust.

Oat Flour Crust:

Use certified gluten-free oat flour to make a gluten-free crust. Mix oat flour with melted butter or a dairy-free alternative and a sweetener of your choice. Press the mixture into the bottom of the springform pan to create a gluten-free oat flour crust.

These gluten-free crust alternatives provide a wonderful foundation for your cheesecake while ensuring that individuals following a gluten-free diet can still enjoy this beloved dessert.

11.2 Grain-Free Cheesecake Variations

If you're looking for grain-free alternatives for your cheesecake, there are several options that offer unique and delicious flavors. Here are a few grain-free cheesecake variations to consider:

Coconut Flour Cheesecake:

Coconut flour is a versatile grain-free option that can be used in cheesecake crusts and fillings. It adds a subtle coconut flavor and a light texture. Combine coconut flour, melted butter or a dairy-free alternative, and a sweetener of your choice to create a grain-free crust. For the filling, use a traditional cheesecake recipe with the addition of coconut flour to achieve a delightful grain-free variation.

Nut Crusts:

Replace traditional crusts with a variety of nut-based options. Crush nuts, such as almonds, pecans, or walnuts, and combine them with melted butter or a dairy-free alternative and a sweetener of your choice. Press the mixture into the bottom of the pan to create a delicious and grain-free crust. Nut crusts offer a rich and flavorful base for your cheesecake.

Seed Crusts:

Explore seed-based crusts for a unique twist. Crush seeds like sunflower seeds, pumpkin seeds, or chia seeds and combine them with melted butter or a dairy-free alternative and a sweetener of your choice. Press the mixture into the bottom of the pan to create a grain-free crust with a delightful nutty flavor.

These grain-free cheesecake variations provide an excellent alternative for individuals looking to avoid grains while still enjoying the indulgence of cheesecake. Experiment with different flavors and textures to find your favorite grain-free combination.

By incorporating gluten-free crust alternatives such as almond flour or gluten-free cookies and exploring grain-free cheesecake variations using coconut flour, nut crusts, or seed crusts, you can enjoy cheesecake while adhering to your dietary needs and preferences. These alternatives offer delicious and satisfying options for those avoiding gluten or grains.

Chapter 12: Cheesecake for Breakfast and Brunch

In Chapter 12, we'll explore the delightful world of cheesecake-inspired breakfast and brunch dishes. Who says you can't enjoy cheesecake in the morning? We'll delve into mouthwatering recipes such as cheesecake-stuffed French toast, cheesecake-filled crepes, and cheesecake-inspired breakfast bowls and smoothies that will add a touch of indulgence to your morning routine. Get ready to start your day with a delicious cheesecake twist!

12.1 Cheesecake-Stuffed French Toast

Combine the decadence of cheesecake with the classic appeal of French toast for a breakfast treat that is sure to delight. Here's an overview of how to make cheesecake-stuffed French toast:

Ingredients:

- 8 slices of bread (choose your favorite type)
- 8 oz cream cheese, softened
- 1/4 cup powdered sugar
- 1 teaspoon vanilla extract
- 4 large eggs
- 1/2 cup milk (dairy or non-dairy)
- Butter or cooking spray for greasing the pan
- Optional toppings: Fresh berries, maple syrup, powdered sugar

Instructions:

1. In a mixing bowl, combine the softened cream cheese, powdered sugar, and vanilla extract. Mix until smooth and well combined.

2. Spread a generous amount of the cream cheese mixture onto one slice of bread. Place another slice of bread on top to create a sandwich. Repeat with the remaining bread slices and cream cheese mixture.

3. In a shallow dish, whisk together the eggs and milk until well combined.

4. Heat a large skillet or griddle over medium heat and grease it with butter or cooking spray.

5. Dip each stuffed bread sandwich into the egg mixture, ensuring both sides are coated.

6. Place the dipped sandwiches onto the heated skillet or griddle. Cook for 2-3 minutes per side, or until golden brown and the cream cheese filling is warm and slightly melted.

7. Remove from the skillet and serve the cheesecake-stuffed French toast warm.

8. Optional: Top with fresh berries, a drizzle of maple syrup, or a sprinkle of powdered sugar for added sweetness.

Cheesecake-stuffed French toast is a delightful breakfast or brunch dish that combines the flavors of creamy cheesecake and warm French toast. It's perfect for a special weekend treat or when you want to indulge in a decadent morning meal.

12.2 Cheesecake-Filled Crepes

Crepes are thin and delicate pancakes that provide the perfect vessel for a luscious cheesecake filling. Here's an overview of how to make cheesecake-filled crepes:

Ingredients:

For the crepes:

- 1 cup all-purpose flour (or gluten-free flour for a gluten-free option)
- 2 tablespoons granulated sugar
- 1/4 teaspoon salt

- 2 large eggs
- 1 cup milk (dairy or non-dairy)
- 2 tablespoons melted butter or oil

For the cheesecake filling:

- 8 oz cream cheese, softened
- 1/4 cup powdered sugar
- 1 teaspoon vanilla extract

Instructions:

For the crepes:

1. In a mixing bowl, whisk together the flour, sugar, and salt.
2. In a separate bowl, whisk the eggs, milk, and melted butter or oil until well combined.
3. Gradually pour the wet ingredients into the dry ingredients, whisking continuously until a smooth batter forms. Let the batter rest for 10-15 minutes.
4. Heat a non-stick skillet or crepe pan over medium heat. Lightly grease the pan with butter or cooking spray.
5. Pour approximately 1/4 cup of the crepe batter onto the heated skillet, tilting and swirling the pan to evenly coat the surface.
6. Cook the crepe for about 1-2 minutes, or until the edges start to turn golden brown. Flip the crepe and cook for another 1-2 minutes on the other side.
7. Transfer the cooked crepe to a plate and repeat the process with the remaining batter, stacking the cooked crepes on top of each other.

For the cheesecake filling:

1. In a mixing bowl, beat the softened cream cheese, powdered sugar, and vanilla extract until smooth and well combined.

Assembly:

1. Take a cooked crepe and spread a generous amount of cheesecake filling on one half of the crepe.
2. Fold the crepe in half to enclose the filling, then fold it in half again to create a triangle or roll it up.
3. Repeat with the remaining crepes and cheesecake filling.

Cheesecake-filled crepes are a delightful and elegant option for breakfast or brunch. Serve them with a dusting of powdered sugar, fresh fruit, or a drizzle of chocolate sauce for added decadence.

12.3 Cheesecake-Inspired Breakfast Bowls and Smoothies

For a lighter take on cheesecake-inspired breakfast options, consider creating breakfast bowls or smoothies with the flavors reminiscent of cheesecake. Here are a few ideas:

Cheesecake Breakfast Bowl:

Blend together frozen berries, a ripe banana, a scoop of dairy or non-dairy yogurt, a splash of milk (dairy or non-dairy), and a tablespoon of nut butter or cream cheese. Top the bowl with granola, fresh berries, and a sprinkle of nuts for added crunch.

Cheesecake Smoothie:

In a blender, combine frozen mixed berries, a ripe banana, a scoop of dairy or non-dairy yogurt, a splash of milk (dairy or non-dairy), a tablespoon of almond butter or cream cheese, and a drizzle of honey or maple syrup. Blend until smooth and creamy. Serve in a glass with a straw or pour it into a bowl and top with a sprinkle of granola and fresh berries.

These cheesecake-inspired breakfast bowls and smoothies are refreshing, nutritious, and packed with flavors reminiscent of the classic dessert. They're a fantastic way to start your day on a sweet and satisfying note.

With cheesecake-stuffed French toast, cheesecake-filled crepes, and cheesecake-inspired breakfast bowls and smoothies, you can elevate your breakfast or brunch experience with the delightful flavors of cheesecake.

These recipes are perfect for special occasions or when you want to treat yourself to a luxurious morning meal.

Chapter 13: Cheesecake-Inspired Beverages

In Chapter 13, we'll explore a delightful array of cheesecake-inspired beverages that are perfect for indulging in the flavors of cheesecake in liquid form. From creamy coffee and lattes to decadent martinis and cocktails, as well as refreshing milkshakes and smoothies, these beverages will satisfy your cheesecake cravings in a delightful and sip-worthy way. Let's dive into the world of cheesecake-inspired drinks!

13.1 Cheesecake-Flavored Coffee and Lattes

Start your day with a delightful cheesecake twist to your morning coffee or latte. Here's an overview of how to make cheesecake-flavored coffee and lattes:

Ingredients:

- Freshly brewed coffee or espresso
- Milk (dairy or non-dairy)
- Cheesecake-flavored syrup or sauce (store-bought or homemade)
- Whipped cream (optional)
- Crumbled graham crackers (optional)

Instructions:

1. Brew your favorite coffee or espresso as per your usual method.
2. In a saucepan, heat the milk over medium heat until hot but not boiling. If desired, froth the milk using a frother or by vigorously whisking it.
3. Add a generous amount of cheesecake-flavored syrup or sauce to your brewed coffee or espresso, stirring well to incorporate

the flavor.

4. Pour the hot milk over the flavored coffee or espresso, leaving room at the top for optional whipped cream.

5. Optional: Top with a dollop of whipped cream and sprinkle crumbled graham crackers on top for added cheesecake-like texture and presentation.

6. Enjoy your cheesecake-flavored coffee or latte as a delightful morning pick-me-up or as a special treat throughout the day.

13.2 Cheesecake Martinis and Cocktails

Elevate your cocktail game with cheesecake-inspired martinis and cocktails. Here's an overview of how to make cheesecake martinis and cocktails:

Ingredients:

- 1 1/2 ounces vodka
- 1 ounce cream liqueur (such as Baileys or a dairy-free alternative)
- 1/2 ounce cheesecake-flavored syrup or liqueur
- Ice
- Graham cracker crumbs for rimming the glass (optional)
- Fresh berries for garnish (optional)

Instructions:

1. Rim a chilled martini glass with graham cracker crumbs by dipping the rim in water or a sweetener syrup and then into the crumbs, rotating to coat evenly (optional).
2. In a cocktail shaker, combine vodka, cream liqueur, cheesecake-flavored syrup or liqueur, and a handful of ice.
3. Shake vigorously until well chilled.
4. Strain the mixture into the prepared martini glass.
5. Optional: Garnish with fresh berries for a pop of color and added freshness.
6. Sip and savor your cheesecake martini or cocktail as a luxurious and decadent treat for special occasions or when you want to indulge in a cocktail with the flavors of cheesecake.

13.3 Cheesecake Milkshakes and Smoothies

For a refreshing and creamy twist on cheesecake, try making cheesecake milkshakes or smoothies. Here's an overview of how to make cheesecake milkshakes and smoothies:

Ingredients:

- 8 oz cream cheese or dairy-free cream cheese alternative
- 1 cup milk (dairy or non-dairy)
- 1 cup ice cream (cheesecake-flavored or vanilla)
- Sweetener of your choice (e.g., honey, maple syrup, agave nectar)
- Optional add-ins: Fresh or frozen berries, crushed graham crackers, whipped cream

Instructions:

1. In a blender, combine cream cheese, milk, ice cream, and sweetener of your choice.
2. Blend until smooth and creamy.
3. Optional: Add fresh or frozen berries, crushed graham crackers, or other desired add-ins to the blender and pulse briefly to incorporate.
4. Pour the milkshake or smoothie into a glass.
5. Optional: Top with a dollop of whipped cream and garnish with crushed graham crackers or fresh berries.
6. Sip and enjoy your cheesecake milkshake or smoothie as a delightful and refreshing beverage to cool down on a hot day or as a tasty treat any time you're in the mood for a creamy and fruity indulgence.

With cheesecake-flavored coffee and lattes, cheesecake martinis and cocktails, as well as cheesecake milkshakes and smoothies, you can enjoy the flavors of cheesecake in a liquid form. These beverages are perfect for special occasions, entertaining guests, or when you simply want to treat yourself to a delightful cheesecake-inspired drink.

Chapter 14: Cheesecake for Kids and Family-Friendly Treats

In Chapter 14, we'll dive into the world of kid-friendly and family-friendly cheesecake treats. These recipes are designed to delight children and the whole family with their miniatures, fun shapes, and colorful presentations. From miniature cheesecake popsicles to cheesecake-filled cupcakes and creative desserts that will capture the imagination of little ones, let's explore these delightful treats!

14.1 Miniature Cheesecake Popsicles

Transform classic cheesecake into a fun and refreshing treat on a stick with miniature cheesecake popsicles. Here's an overview of how to make them:

Ingredients:

- 8 oz cream cheese, softened
- 1/2 cup powdered sugar
- 1 teaspoon vanilla extract
- 1/2 cup heavy cream or whipped topping
- Fresh fruit or cookie crumbs for topping (optional)
- Popsicle molds and sticks

Instructions:

1. In a mixing bowl, beat the softened cream cheese until smooth.
2. Add the powdered sugar and vanilla extract to the cream cheese

and continue beating until well combined.

3. In a separate bowl, whip the heavy cream or use pre-made whipped topping until stiff peaks form.

4. Gently fold the whipped cream into the cream cheese mixture until well incorporated.

5. Pour the mixture into popsicle molds, leaving a little space at the top for expansion.

6. Insert popsicle sticks into each mold.

7. Optional: Sprinkle fresh fruit pieces or cookie crumbs on top of each popsicle for added flavor and texture.

8. Freeze the popsicles for at least 4 hours or until completely set.

9. To remove the popsicles from the molds, briefly run the molds under warm water to loosen the popsicles.

Miniature cheesecake popsicles are a fun and refreshing treat for kids and the whole family. The creamy and sweet flavor of cheesecake combined with the novelty of a popsicle is sure to be a hit.

14.2 Cheesecake-Filled Cupcakes

Surprise your little ones with a delightful surprise hidden inside cupcakes – a luscious cheesecake filling! Here's an overview of how to make cheesecake-filled cupcakes:

Ingredients:

For the cupcakes:

- Your favorite cupcake recipe or a boxed mix

For the cheesecake filling:

- 8 oz cream cheese, softened
- 1/4 cup granulated sugar
- 1 egg
- 1/2 teaspoon vanilla extract

Instructions:

1. Preheat the oven according to your cupcake recipe or boxed mix instructions. Line a cupcake pan with cupcake liners.
2. Prepare the cupcake batter according to your recipe or boxed mix instructions.
3. In a separate bowl, beat the softened cream cheese, granulated sugar, egg, and vanilla extract until smooth and well combined.
4. Fill each cupcake liner halfway with the cupcake batter.
5. Spoon a tablespoon of the cheesecake filling into the center of each cupcake.
6. Cover the cheesecake filling with more cupcake batter until the cupcake liners are about 2/3 full.
7. Bake the cupcakes according to your recipe or boxed mix instructions, until a toothpick inserted into the cupcakes comes out clean.
8. Let the cupcakes cool completely before frosting or decorating as desired.

When your little ones take a bite into these cupcakes, they'll be pleasantly surprised by the creamy and delicious cheesecake filling hidden inside!

14.3 Fun and Colorful Cheesecake Desserts for Kids

Make cheesecake even more appealing to kids with fun and colorful presentations. Here are a few ideas:

Cheesecake Parfaits: Layer crumbled cookies, colorful fruits like berries or sliced bananas, and dollops of cheesecake filling in clear cups or jars to create visually appealing and delicious cheesecake parfaits.

Rainbow Cheesecake Bars: Create a colorful twist by dividing the cheesecake batter into portions and coloring each portion with different food coloring. Layer the colored batters in a baking dish and swirl them together before baking to achieve vibrant and eye-catching rainbow cheesecake bars.

Cheesecake Dip with Fruit Skewers: Prepare a creamy and sweet cheesecake dip using cream cheese, powdered sugar, and vanilla extract. Serve it with skewers loaded with fresh fruit pieces for a fun and interactive dipping experience.

These fun and colorful cheesecake desserts will capture the imagination of kids and make cheesecake a delightful treat for the whole family.

With miniature cheesecake popsicles, cheesecake-filled cupcakes, and fun and colorful cheesecake desserts, you can bring the joy of cheesecake to the youngest members of your family. These treats are not only delicious but also visually appealing and engaging, making them perfect for parties, special occasions, or simply enjoying a sweet moment with your kids.

Chapter 15: Light and Healthy Cheesecake Options

In Chapter 15, we'll explore light and healthy alternatives to traditional cheesecakes. These options are perfect for those who want to enjoy the flavors of cheesecake while opting for lighter and healthier versions. From low-fat New York cheesecake to Greek yogurt-based cheesecakes and fruit-infused, naturally sweetened alternatives, let's discover these delicious and health-conscious options.

15.1 Low-Fat New York Cheesecake

Indulge in the classic flavors of New York cheesecake while reducing the fat content with a low-fat version. Here's an overview of how to make a low-fat New York cheesecake:

Ingredients:
For the crust:

- 1 1/2 cups graham cracker crumbs
- 3 tablespoons melted butter or a lighter butter alternative

For the filling:

- 16 oz low-fat cream cheese
- 1 cup low-fat Greek yogurt
- 3/4 cup granulated sugar or a natural sweetener alternative
- 3 large eggs
- 1 teaspoon vanilla extract
- 2 tablespoons all-purpose flour or a gluten-free flour alternative

Instructions:

1. Preheat the oven to 325°F (163°C). Grease a springform pan and line the bottom with parchment paper.
2. In a bowl, combine the graham cracker crumbs and melted butter. Mix until the crumbs are evenly coated. Press the crumb mixture into the bottom of the prepared springform pan to create the crust.
3. In a mixing bowl, beat the low-fat cream cheese until smooth and creamy.
4. Add the Greek yogurt, granulated sugar or natural sweetener, eggs, vanilla extract, and flour to the cream cheese. Beat until well combined and smooth.
5. Pour the filling onto the crust in the springform pan, spreading it evenly.
6. Bake for approximately 50-60 minutes, or until the top is set but still slightly jiggly.
7. Remove from the oven and let it cool in the pan for about 10 minutes. Then, transfer it to a wire rack to cool completely.
8. Once cooled, refrigerate the cheesecake for at least 4 hours or overnight before serving.

Low-fat New York cheesecake allows you to enjoy the classic flavors and textures of cheesecake while reducing the fat content. It's a lighter option that still delivers on taste.

15.2 Greek Yogurt-Based Cheesecakes

Incorporate the tangy and creamy goodness of Greek yogurt into your cheesecake for a lighter and protein-packed option. Here's an overview of how to make Greek yogurt-based cheesecakes:

Ingredients:
For the crust:

- 1 1/2 cups graham cracker crumbs
- 3 tablespoons melted butter or a lighter butter alternative

For the filling:

- 16 oz cream cheese or a lighter cream cheese alternative, softened
- 1 cup plain Greek yogurt
- 3/4 cup granulated sugar or a natural sweetener alternative
- 3 large eggs
- 1 teaspoon vanilla extract
- 2 tablespoons all-purpose flour or a gluten-free flour alternative

Instructions:

1. Preheat the oven to 325°F (163°C). Grease a springform pan and line the bottom with parchment paper.
2. In a bowl, combine the graham cracker crumbs and melted butter. Mix until the crumbs are evenly coated. Press the crumb mixture into the bottom of the prepared springform pan to create the crust.
3. In a mixing bowl, beat the cream cheese or lighter cream cheese alternative until smooth and creamy.
4. Add the Greek yogurt, granulated sugar or natural sweetener, eggs, vanilla extract, and flour to the cream cheese. Beat until well combined and smooth.
5. Pour the filling onto the crust in the springform pan, spreading it evenly.
6. Bake for approximately 50-60 minutes, or until the top is set but still slightly jiggly.
7. Remove from the oven and let it cool in the pan for about 10 minutes. Then, transfer it to a wire rack to cool completely.
8. Once cooled, refrigerate the cheesecake for at least 4 hours or

overnight before serving.

Greek yogurt-based cheesecakes offer a tangy and creamy twist to traditional cheesecake while providing a protein boost and reducing the overall fat content.

15.3 Fruit-Infused and Naturally Sweetened Cheesecake Alternatives

Infuse your cheesecakes with the natural sweetness and flavors of fruits for a healthier twist. Here's an overview of how to make fruit-infused and naturally sweetened cheesecake alternatives:

Ingredients:

For the crust:

- 1 1/2 cups graham cracker crumbs or a gluten-free alternative
- 3 tablespoons melted butter or a lighter butter alternative

For the filling:

- 16 oz cream cheese or a lighter cream cheese alternative, softened
- 1 cup fruit puree or mashed fruit (such as berries, mango, or citrus)
- 1/2 cup natural sweetener (such as honey, maple syrup, or agave nectar)
- 3 large eggs
- 1 teaspoon vanilla extract
- 2 tablespoons all-purpose flour or a gluten-free flour alternative

Instructions:

1. Preheat the oven to 325°F (163°C). Grease a springform pan and line the bottom with parchment paper.
2. In a bowl, combine the graham cracker crumbs and melted butter. Mix until the crumbs are evenly coated. Press the crumb

mixture into the bottom of the prepared springform pan to create the crust.

3. In a mixing bowl, beat the cream cheese or lighter cream cheese alternative until smooth and creamy.

4. Add the fruit puree or mashed fruit and natural sweetener to the cream cheese. Mix until well combined.

5. Add the eggs, vanilla extract, and flour to the cream cheese mixture. Beat until smooth and creamy.

6. Pour the filling onto the crust in the springform pan, spreading it evenly.

7. Bake for approximately 50-60 minutes, or until the top is set but still slightly jiggly.

8. Remove from the oven and let it cool in the pan for about 10 minutes. Then, transfer it to a wire rack to cool completely.

9. Once cooled, refrigerate the cheesecake for at least 4 hours or overnight before serving.

Fruit-infused and naturally sweetened cheesecake alternatives offer a healthier option by incorporating the natural sweetness of fruits and reducing the need for additional sugar or sweeteners.

With low-fat New York cheesecake, Greek yogurt-based cheesecakes, and fruit-infused, naturally sweetened cheesecake alternatives, you can enjoy lighter and healthier versions of this beloved dessert. These options provide a satisfying and guilt-free indulgence while still delivering on flavor.

Chapter 16: Cheesecake Baking Techniques and Troubleshooting

In Chapter 16, we'll explore various baking techniques and troubleshooting tips to help you achieve perfect cheesecakes every time. We'll cover the water bath baking method for even cooking, preventing cracks and sinking in the middle of your cheesecake, and rescuing and fixing common cheesecake mishaps. Let's dive into these essential techniques and tips!

16.1 Water Bath Baking Method for Even Cooking

The water bath baking method is a technique used to ensure gentle and even heat distribution during the baking process, which helps prevent cheesecakes from overcooking or cracking. Here's an overview of how to use the water bath baking method:

1. Preheat your oven according to the recipe instructions.
2. Wrap the bottom and sides of your springform pan with aluminum foil to prevent water from seeping into the cheesecake.
3. Place your prepared cheesecake in the center of a larger baking pan or roasting pan.
4. Carefully pour hot water into the larger pan, ensuring that the water reaches about halfway up the sides of the springform pan.
5. Place the water bath and the cheesecake in the preheated oven and bake according to the recipe instructions.

The water bath creates a moist and gentle cooking environment, helping to prevent cracks and achieve a smooth, creamy texture in your cheesecake. It's an essential technique for baking perfect cheesecakes.

16.2 Preventing Cracks and Sinking in the Middle

1. Cracks and sinking in the middle are common issues that can occur while baking cheesecakes. Here are some tips to help prevent these problems:

2. Use room temperature ingredients: Ensure that all your ingredients, especially the cream cheese and eggs, are at room temperature before mixing. This allows for smoother blending and reduces the risk of overmixing, which can lead to cracks.

3. Avoid overmixing: Mix the ingredients just until they are well combined. Overmixing can introduce too much air into the batter, which can contribute to cracks and sinking.

4. Bake at a lower temperature: Consider baking your cheesecake at a slightly lower temperature than the recipe suggests. Lower temperatures can help prevent the top from setting too quickly and reduce the risk of cracks.

5. Don't open the oven door during baking: Opening the oven door can cause sudden temperature changes and drafts, which can lead to cracks and sinking. Keep the oven door closed during the baking process.

6. Gradually cool the cheesecake: After baking, turn off the oven and let the cheesecake cool gradually in the oven for about an hour. This gradual cooling process helps minimize sudden temperature changes that can cause cracking.

Implementing these preventive measures can greatly reduce the chances of cracks and sinking in the middle of your cheesecake, resulting in a picture-perfect dessert.

16.3 Rescuing and Fixing Common Cheesecake Mishaps

Sometimes, despite our best efforts, unexpected mishaps can occur while baking cheesecakes. Here are some common cheesecake mishaps and tips for rescuing and fixing them:

Cracks: If cracks do appear on the surface of your cheesecake, don't worry! You can easily fix them by gently spreading a thin layer of sour cream or a sweetened sour cream topping over the cracks. This will create a smooth and creamy appearance.

Sinking in the middle: If your cheesecake sinks in the middle after baking, it's likely due to undercooking. To rescue it, return the cheesecake to the oven and bake for an additional 5-10 minutes. Keep a close eye on it and remove it from the oven when the center is set but still slightly jiggly. Avoid overcooking, as it can lead to a dry texture.

Sticky or undercooked center: If your cheesecake has a sticky or undercooked center, it might need additional baking time. Cover the top of the cheesecake with aluminum foil to prevent over-browning, and continue baking in 5-minute intervals until the center is set. Be cautious not to overbake.

Crumbly texture: A crumbly texture can occur if the cheesecake is overcooked or has been overmixed. To salvage it, serve the cheesecake chilled and consider topping it with sauces, fruits, or whipped cream to enhance the overall experience.

These rescue techniques can help salvage common cheesecake mishaps and ensure you still have a delicious and enjoyable dessert to serve.

By utilizing the water bath baking method for even cooking, implementing preventive measures to prevent cracks and sinking, and knowing how to rescue and fix common cheesecake mishaps, you'll be well-equipped to tackle any baking challenges and achieve beautiful, flawless cheesecakes.

Chapter 17: Cheesecake Storage and Freezing Tips

In Chapter 17, we'll delve into the essential tips for storing and freezing cheesecakes. Proper storage techniques are crucial to maintaining the freshness and quality of your cheesecakes, while freezing can be a convenient option for preserving them for future enjoyment. We'll also cover how to thaw and revive frozen cheesecakes for optimal taste and texture. Let's explore these tips for cheesecake storage and freezing!

17.1 Proper Storage Techniques to Maintain Freshness

To maintain the freshness and quality of your cheesecake, proper storage techniques are key. Here are some tips:

Refrigeration: Cheesecakes should be stored in the refrigerator to prevent spoilage. Once the cheesecake has cooled completely, cover it loosely with plastic wrap or place it in an airtight container. This will help prevent moisture loss and keep the cheesecake from absorbing odors in the fridge.

Shelf Life: Most cheesecakes can be refrigerated for 3-5 days. However, it's important to note that the texture and flavor may change slightly over time.

Avoid Direct Air Exposure: When storing your cheesecake in the refrigerator, make sure it is not directly exposed to circulating air, as this can dry out the surface. If needed, place a dome-shaped lid or cover over the cheesecake to protect it.

Toppings and Sauces: If your cheesecake has toppings or sauces, such as fruit compotes or chocolate ganache, it's best to add them just before serving or as individual servings. This helps maintain their freshness and prevents them from seeping into the cheesecake.

By following these proper storage techniques, you can ensure that your cheesecake remains fresh and delicious for as long as possible.

17.2 Freezing and Thawing Cheesecakes

Freezing cheesecakes can be a convenient way to preserve them for later enjoyment. Here's how to freeze and thaw cheesecakes properly:

Freezing:

1. Ensure that your cheesecake has cooled completely after baking and has been refrigerated for a few hours before freezing. This will help set the texture.

2. Wrap the cheesecake securely in plastic wrap, making sure it is tightly sealed to prevent freezer burn and the absorption of odors.

3. Place the wrapped cheesecake in an airtight container or a heavy-duty freezer bag. Label the container with the date for future reference.

4. Place the cheesecake in the freezer, ideally on a flat surface to maintain its shape.

Thawing:

When ready to enjoy the frozen cheesecake, transfer it from the freezer to the refrigerator. Allow it to thaw gradually in the refrigerator overnight or for approximately 6-8 hours.

After thawing, remove the plastic wrap or container and let the cheesecake come to room temperature on the counter for about 30 minutes to an hour before serving. This will help restore its creamy texture.

It's important to note that freezing and thawing can slightly affect the texture of the cheesecake, and it may not be as firm as when freshly made. However, the taste and overall experience can still be delightful.

17.3 Reviving Frozen Cheesecakes for Optimal Taste and Texture

To revive the taste and texture of a frozen cheesecake, you can take a few additional steps:

Refresh Toppings and Sauces: If your cheesecake has toppings or sauces, consider refreshing them before serving. Add fresh fruit or prepare a new batch of sauces to enhance the presentation and flavor.

Add Garnishes: Just before serving, consider adding fresh garnishes such as mint leaves, chocolate shavings, or a dusting of powdered sugar to elevate the visual appeal.

Serve with Accompaniments: To enhance the overall experience, serve your cheesecake with complementary accompaniments such as whipped cream, fruit coulis, or a scoop of ice cream.

By taking these additional steps, you can revive the flavor, appearance, and overall enjoyment of your frozen cheesecake.

By following proper storage techniques, freezing and thawing methods, and taking additional steps to revive the taste and texture of frozen cheesecakes, you can enjoy your homemade cheesecake even after it has been stored or frozen.

Chapter 18: Cheesecake Garnishes and Decorations

In Chapter 18, we'll explore the art of garnishing and decorating cheesecakes to elevate their visual appeal and add delightful finishing touches. From fresh fruit arrangements and edible flowers to chocolate curls and shavings, as well as creative whipped cream designs and patterns, we'll discover how these decorative elements can transform your cheesecakes into stunning and irresistible desserts. Let's dive into the world of cheesecake garnishes and decorations!

18.1 Fresh Fruit Arrangements and Edible Flowers

Fresh fruit arrangements and edible flowers are a beautiful and vibrant way to garnish and decorate your cheesecakes. Here are some ideas to inspire your creativity:

Berry Medley: Top your cheesecake with a medley of fresh berries such as strawberries, raspberries, blueberries, and blackberries. Arrange them in an aesthetically pleasing pattern, creating a burst of colors and flavors.

Citrus Zest: Add a touch of brightness by grating fresh citrus zest, such as lemon or orange, over the top of your cheesecake. The vibrant zest not only adds visual appeal but also enhances the overall flavor.

Fruit Slices: Thinly slice fruits like kiwi, pineapple, or oranges and arrange them in a decorative pattern on top of the cheesecake. This adds a tropical touch and creates an eye-catching display.

Edible Flowers: Select edible flowers such as pansies, violets, or nasturtiums to adorn your cheesecake. Ensure that the flowers are pesticide-free and suitable for consumption. Gently place them on top of the cheesecake or scatter them around the plate for an elegant and whimsical touch.

These fresh fruit arrangements and edible flowers will add a burst of color and natural beauty to your cheesecake, making it an enticing centerpiece for any occasion.

18.2 Chocolate Curls and Shavings

Chocolate curls and shavings provide a touch of decadence and elegance to cheesecakes. Here's how you can create these delectable chocolate decorations:

Chocolate Curls: Start with a block or bar of high-quality chocolate. Use a vegetable peeler or a sharp knife to carefully scrape the chocolate at a slight angle, creating thin curls. Gently place the curls on top of your cheesecake, creating a visually appealing texture and flavor contrast.

Chocolate Shavings: Using a grater or a microplane, grate the chocolate against its flat side to create delicate chocolate shavings. Sprinkle the shavings over the cheesecake, allowing them to fall gently and cover the surface with a luscious layer of chocolate.

These chocolate curls and shavings add a touch of indulgence and create a stunning presentation, making your cheesecake even more irresistible.

18.3 Creative Whipped Cream Designs and Patterns

Whipped cream is a classic accompaniment to cheesecake, and you can take it to the next level by creating creative designs and patterns. Here are some ideas to inspire you:

Rosettes: Using a piping bag fitted with a star-shaped tip, pipe whipped cream rosettes around the edges of the cheesecake. Create a border of beautiful and uniform swirls that adds elegance and texture.

Waves and Ruffles: Experiment with different piping tips to create waves, ruffles, or other intricate designs with whipped cream. Use your creativity to pipe the cream in various patterns, enhancing the visual appeal of the cheesecake.

Dollops and Dots: For a more playful presentation, use a spoon or a small scoop to place dollops or dots of whipped cream on top of the cheesecake. Arrange them in a random or symmetrical pattern, creating a whimsical and inviting design.

These creative whipped cream designs and patterns allow you to showcase your artistic flair while adding a creamy and delightful element to your cheesecake.

By incorporating fresh fruit arrangements and edible flowers, chocolate curls and shavings, as well as creative whipped cream designs and patterns, you can elevate the visual appeal of your cheesecakes and create stunning desserts that are as beautiful as they are delicious. In the final chapter, we'll reflect on our journey as cheesecake connoisseurs and celebrate the wonderful world of New York cheesecakes.

Chapter 19: Cheesecake Pairings and Serving Suggestions

In Chapter 19, we'll explore the art of pairing and serving cheesecake to create a well-rounded dessert experience. From ideal flavor combinations with cheesecake to cheese and wine pairings, as well as savory accompaniments, we'll discover how to enhance the flavors and create memorable moments with your cheesecake creations. Let's dive into the world of cheesecake pairings and serving suggestions!

19.1 Ideal Flavor Combinations with Cheesecake

Cheesecake offers a rich and creamy base that can be complemented by a variety of flavors. Here are some ideal flavor combinations to consider when serving your cheesecake:

Fruity Delights: Pair your cheesecake with fresh fruits such as strawberries, raspberries, or blueberries. The natural sweetness and tartness of the fruits provide a refreshing contrast to the creamy cheesecake.

Decadent Chocolate: Combine the indulgence of chocolate with your cheesecake. Serve it with a drizzle of chocolate ganache, sprinkle chocolate shavings on top, or create a chocolate crust for a double dose of chocolate goodness.

Nutty Crunch: Add a delightful crunch by incorporating nuts such as toasted almonds, pecans, or walnuts. Sprinkle them over the cheesecake or use them as a crust base for added texture and flavor.

Citrus Zest: Brighten up your cheesecake with a touch of citrus. Sprinkle lemon or orange zest on top of the cheesecake to add a refreshing and tangy note that complements the richness of the cream cheese.

These flavor combinations will enhance the overall experience of your cheesecake and provide a harmonious balance of tastes.

19.2 Cheese and Wine Pairings

Cheese and wine pairings can also be applied to cheesecake to create a delightful combination of flavors. Here are some cheese and wine pairings to consider when serving your cheesecake:

Creamy Cheesecake with Brie: Serve a creamy cheesecake with a slice of Brie cheese. The creamy and buttery texture of the Brie complements the richness of the cheesecake, creating a luxurious flavor profile. Pair it with a Chardonnay or a sparkling wine.

Fruity Cheesecake with Goat Cheese: Pair a fruity cheesecake, such as a raspberry or strawberry-infused variation, with a tangy goat cheese. The tanginess of the goat cheese balances the sweetness of the fruit, creating a dynamic taste experience. Accompany it with a Pinot Noir or a Rosé.

Chocolate Cheesecake with Blue Cheese: Indulge in the decadence of a chocolate cheesecake by pairing it with a crumbly and slightly pungent blue cheese. The bold flavors of the blue cheese complement the richness of the chocolate, creating a delightful contrast. Enjoy it with a Cabernet Sauvignon or a Port wine.

These cheese and wine pairings offer a sophisticated and flavorful combination that elevates the cheesecake experience.

19.3 Savory Accompaniments for a Well-Rounded Dessert Experience

To create a well-rounded dessert experience, consider incorporating savory accompaniments that balance the sweetness of the cheesecake. Here are some ideas:

Salted Caramel Sauce: Drizzle a salted caramel sauce over your cheesecake to add a hint of saltiness and enhance the overall flavor profile.

Spiced Nuts: Serve spiced nuts, such as cinnamon-roasted almonds or candied pecans, alongside your cheesecake. The spices and crunch provide a savory element that complements the creamy sweetness.

Herb-Infused Syrups: Experiment with herb-infused syrups, such as lavender syrup or basil-infused syrup, to add a unique and savory twist to your cheesecake.

These savory accompaniments add depth and complexity to the dessert, creating a well-rounded and memorable experience.

By considering ideal flavor combinations, cheese and wine pairings, and incorporating savory accompaniments, you can elevate the flavors and create a well-rounded dessert experience with your cheesecakes. In the final chapter, we'll wrap up our journey as cheesecake connoisseurs and celebrate the wonderful world of New York cheesecakes.

Chapter 20: Cheesecake-Focused Restaurants and Bakeries in New York

In Chapter 20, we'll explore the cheesecake-focused restaurants and bakeries in New York City, the birthplace of the beloved New York cheesecake. We'll highlight notable cheesecake destinations, provide profiles of renowned cheesecake establishments, and offer insider tips for cheesecake lovers visiting New York. Let's embark on a delicious journey through the cheesecake scene in the Big Apple!

20.1 Notable Cheesecake Destinations in New York City

New York City is renowned for its diverse culinary scene, and cheesecake holds a special place in the city's gastronomy. Here are some notable cheesecake destinations to add to your itinerary:

Junior's Restaurant: Junior's, located in Brooklyn, has been an institution since 1950. Their original New York cheesecake recipe is legendary, known for its rich and creamy texture. Junior's has multiple locations throughout the city, making it easily accessible for cheesecake enthusiasts.

Eileen's Special Cheesecake: Situated in the heart of SoHo, Eileen's Special Cheesecake is a must-visit for cheesecake connoisseurs. Known for their individual-sized cheesecakes, Eileen's offers a wide variety of flavors and toppings to satisfy every palate.

Two Little Red Hens: Nestled on the Upper East Side, Two Little Red Hens is a cozy bakery that takes pride in crafting exceptional cheesecakes. Their classic New York cheesecake is a crowd favorite, with its velvety smooth texture and authentic flavor.

Veniero's Pasticceria & Caffe: Established in 1894, Veniero's is a historic Italian bakery located in the East Village. Alongside their delectable pastries, they offer a delightful array of cheesecakes, including ricotta cheesecake and seasonal variations.

These notable cheesecake destinations in New York City showcase the city's commitment to perfecting the art of cheesecake-making, ensuring that every bite is a slice of culinary heaven.

20.2 Profiles of Renowned Cheesecake Establishments

Let's dive deeper into the profiles of renowned cheesecake establishments in New York City:

Junior's Restaurant:

Location: Multiple locations in Brooklyn and Manhattan

Signature Cheesecake: Junior's Original New York Cheesecake with a sponge cake crust

Insider Tip: Pair your cheesecake with their famous strawberry topping for a classic combination.

Eileen's Special Cheesecake:

Location: 17 Cleveland Place, New York, NY

Signature Cheesecake: Eileen's Original Plain Cheesecake with a buttery graham cracker crust

Insider Tip: Try their seasonal cheesecake flavors, such as pumpkin spice or strawberry-rhubarb, for a unique twist.

Two Little Red Hens:

Location: 1652 2nd Avenue, New York, NY

Signature Cheesecake: Classic New York Cheesecake with a smooth and creamy texture

Insider Tip: Arrive early to ensure a wide selection of flavors, as Two Little Red Hens' cheesecakes are in high demand.

Veniero's Pasticceria & Caffe:

Location: 342 East 11th Street, New York, NY

Signature Cheesecake: Traditional Italian Ricotta Cheesecake

Insider Tip: Explore their other Italian pastries and desserts while visiting, as Veniero's offers a diverse selection of sweet treats.

20.3 Insider Tips for Cheesecake Lovers Visiting New York

If you're a cheesecake lover planning a visit to New York City, here are some insider tips to enhance your cheesecake experience:

Explore Neighborhood Bakeries: While the renowned establishments are a must-visit, don't overlook the smaller neighborhood bakeries. They often have hidden gems and unique cheesecake variations that offer a local touch.

Check Seasonal Offerings: Keep an eye out for seasonal cheesecake flavors and limited-time specials. Many bakeries introduce unique creations to celebrate holidays and the changing seasons, offering a chance to savor something new and exciting.

Take a Cheesecake Tour: Consider joining a cheesecake-focused food tour that takes you on a culinary journey through the city's best cheesecake destinations. It's a fun and informative way to sample a variety of cheesecakes while learning about their history and cultural significance.

Pair with Local Delights: New York City is a melting pot of cuisines. Pair your cheesecake experience with other local delights, such as a classic hot dog from a street vendor or a slice of New York-style pizza. Embrace the city's culinary diversity and create a memorable food adventure.

Share and Indulge: Cheesecake is best enjoyed with good company. Invite friends or fellow cheesecake enthusiasts to join you on your tasting adventures, allowing you to sample a wider variety of flavors and share the joy of indulging in this iconic dessert.

By following these insider tips, you'll be able to navigate the cheesecake scene in New York City like a true aficionado, savoring the best the city has to offer.

As we wrap up our journey through the world of New York cheesecakes, we hope you've gained a deeper appreciation for this delectable dessert. From mastering the art of making New York cheesecakes to exploring flavor variations, decorating techniques, and the vibrant cheesecake scene in New York City, you are now equipped to embark on your own cheesecake adventures. Enjoy the creamy, indulgent, and utterly delicious world of New York cheesecakes!

In this comprehensive cookbook dedicated to New York Cheesecake, we embarked on a flavorful journey through the history, techniques, and delicious variations of this iconic dessert. From understanding the origins of New York cheesecake to mastering the art of creating a perfect creamy texture, we covered everything you need to know to become a skilled cheesecake connoisseur.

Each chapter offered a unique perspective on the world of cheesecake, including classic recipes, creative variations, delectable toppings and sauces, and even savory adaptations. We explored different ways to serve and present cheesecakes, from individual portions to special occasion centerpieces. Additionally, we delved into the world of vegan, gluten-free, and dairy-free alternatives, ensuring that everyone can indulge in the delight of New York cheesecake.

We also provided insights into storing, freezing, and reviving cheesecakes, as well as tips for decorating with garnishes, creating artistic designs, and pairing cheesecake with complementary flavors, cheeses, wines, and accompaniments.

To top it off, we took a virtual tour of New York City's renowned cheesecake destinations, highlighting notable establishments and providing insider tips for cheesecake lovers visiting the Big Apple. Whether you choose to sample the offerings at Junior's, Eileen's Special Cheesecake, Two Little Red Hens, or Veniero's Pasticceria & Caffe, you're guaranteed a memorable and delicious experience.

Now armed with the knowledge and recipes from this New York Cheesecake Cookbook, you have the tools to create mouthwatering cheesecakes in your own kitchen and impress family and friends with your culinary skills. So go forth, explore the endless possibilities, and savor the creamy indulgence of New York cheesecake. Happy baking!